# Eternity Today

# Eternity Today

Selected Poems by KU SANG


Back cover illustration by Kang Hyung-koo
Printed in Seoul, Korea

First Published in May 2005
By Seoul Selection
B1 Korean Publishers Association Bldg., 105-2 Sagan-dong, Jongno-gu, Seoul 110-190, Korea
Tel 82-2-734-9567/8
Fax 82-2-734-9562
www.seoulselection.com



ISBN 89-953760-6-6 03810

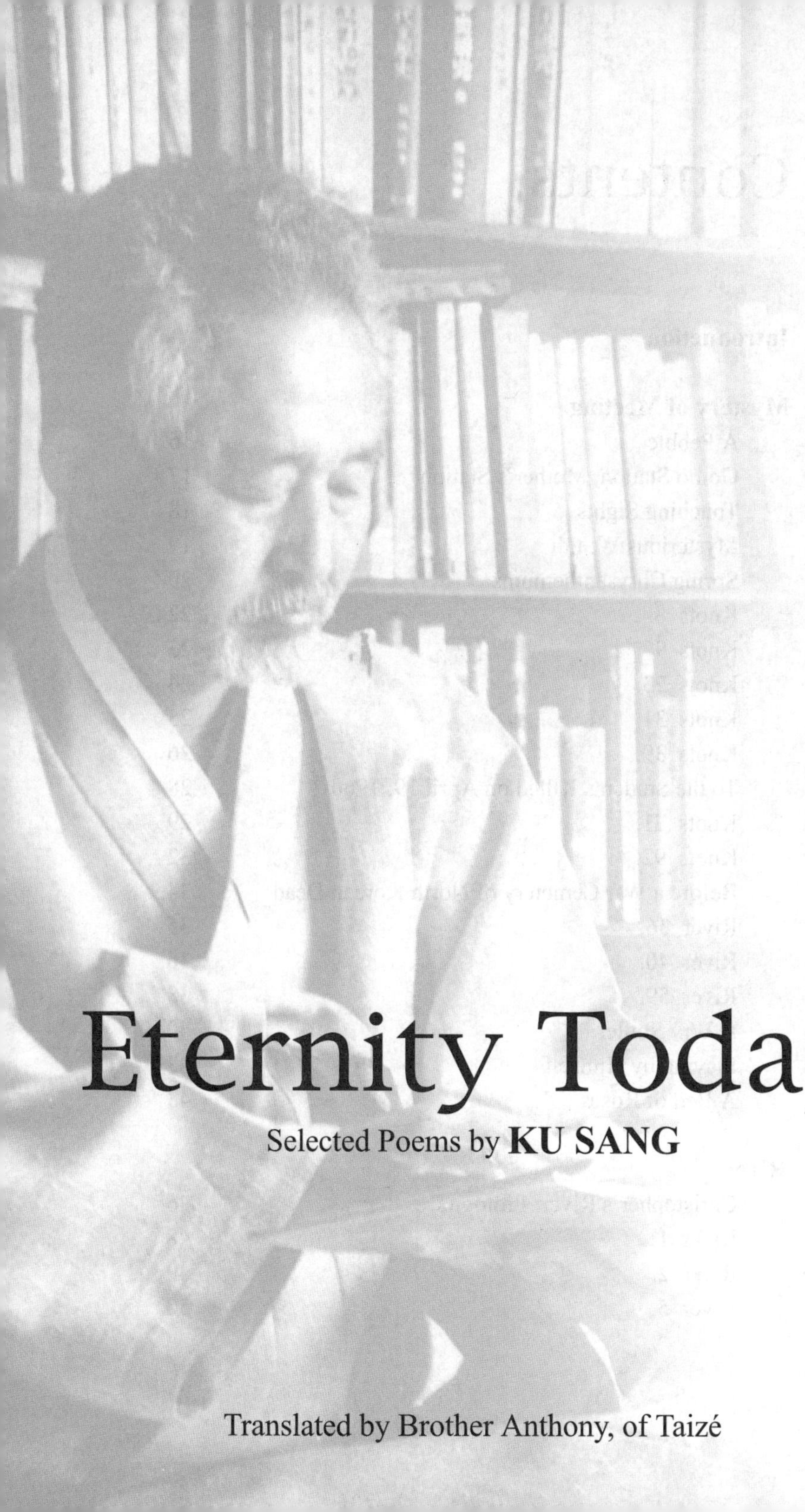

# Eternity Today

Selected Poems by **KU SANG**

Translated by Brother Anthony, of Taizé

# Contents

These translations were first published in:
*Wastelands of Fire* (Forest Books, London, 1990) reprinted in a bilingual edition by DapGae (Seoul, 2000) with the title *Wasteland Poems*.
*River and Fields: A Korean Century* (Forest Books, London, 1991)
*Infant Splendor* (Samseong Publishing, Seoul, 1990)
*Even the Knots on Quince Trees Tell Tales* (DapGae, Seoul, 2004)

The poems in Ku Sang's large cycles have no titles but are simply numbered.
River: *Christopher's River* (60 poems)
Fields: *Diary of the Fields* (60 poems)
Knots: *Even the Knots on Quince Trees Tell Tales* (100 poems)

# Introduction

In 1946, Ku Sang took leave of his widowed mother, who was living near Wonsan, on the east coast of what is now North Korea. As she watched from the road in front of the gateway, he walked away, heading for the southern part of the Korean peninsula. Neither could imagine that they would never meet again. After returning from studies of comparative religion in Tokyo a few years earlier, he had found work as a journalist and had already written a number of poems. With other local poets, he had recently been working on a collective volume of their poems, to be entitled *Eunghyang* 'Congealed fragrance.' Before any book could be published, it had to be approved by the authorities, already dominated by the Communist party, and in this case the censors had detected seven separate serious ideological failings. To avoid a trial and a potentially lethal outcome, Ku Sang fled, leaving behind not only his mother and his elder brother, a Catholic priest, but also his recently married wife. His wife was later able to join him in the South, but the other members of his family remained in the North until their deaths.

That man, the most highly respected, senior Korean poet Ku Sang, died in Seoul on Tuesday May 11, 2004, at the age of 85. He was born in Seoul on September 16, 1919, but when he was only a small child his family moved to the north-eastern city of Wonsan, where he grew up. Ku Sang underwent a crisis of faith during his student years in Japan, where he studied the philosophy of religion, especially Buddhism; later he slowly found his own understanding of Catholicism, thanks in part to the works of French Catholic philosophers such as Jacques Maritain and Gabriel Marcel. He frequently insisted that without a clearly-thought metaphysical system, there could be no truth and no true poetry. It was this that inspired Cardinal Kim Su-hwan, the retired Archbishop of Seoul, to say of Ku Sang during his sermon at the funeral Mass, 'He was truly a Catholic poet, not just in the sense that he belonged to the Catholic Church and respected its doctrines, but in the sense that his heart was universal, that his poems had a vision that was cosmic, touching people in every corner of the world.'

Once he safely reached South Korea in 1946, he soon found work writing for newspapers, then served in a military intelligence unit during the Korean War (1950-3). After that, he returned to journalism and wrote articles and opinion columns, then editorial columns, for various newspapers. Soon after the Korean War ended, in 1953, when the president Syngman Rhee was clearly abusing his powers, Ku Sang wrote a series of articles 'Democratic Accusations,' attacking the corruption of his regime. He was immediately imprisoned on trumped-up charges for several months. He lived for many years in Waegwan, not far from Daegu, where his wife ran a children's hospital while Ku Sang worked as a journalist especially connected with the *Gyeonghyang Shinmun*, then run by the Catholic church. After the 1961 coup by Park Chung-hee, whom Ku Sang had come to know several years before, he was pressured to accept a ministerial position and finally, to avoid this, he arranged to spend several years in charge of the newspaper's Tokyo bureau. Later he lectured on literature in a number of universities, including Chung-Ang University in Anseong, and made two lengthy visits as a visiting professor to the East-West Center at the University of Hawaii.

In the course of his life, Ku Sang published a number of volumes of poetry, as well as essays on social, literary, and spiritual topics; he also wrote plays and scenarios, and edited some popular anthologies. His first volume, 'Ku Sang,' was published in 1951. A volume of the poems he wrote on the sufferings of the Korean people during the war and its aftermath, *Chotoeui shi* 'Wastelands of Fire,' was published in 1956 and attracted considerable attention. He then turned toward nature and began the first of his great cycles, *Bat ilgi* 'Diary of the Fields' which was first published in 1967. This was later joined by a second cycle, *Christopherui gang* 'Christopher's River,' inspired by his daily walks along the banks of the Han River in Seoul and both express the spiritual, social and ecological values he discovered in Nature.

Later, he published essays on specifically Catholic themes in such volumes as 'Jesus of Nazareth' (1979) and religious poems in *Malsseumui shilsang* 'The True Appearance of the Word' (1980). In 1981, his work took on a more overtly satiric tone with his denunciations of the materialism and emptiness of modern life in the poems of *Ggamagui* 'The Crow.' The volume *Mogwa ongduriedo sayeoni itta* 'Even the knots on quince trees tell tales' first published in 1984 and subsequently extended contains 100 poems evoking his life's often uncertain and sometimes amusingly stumbling progress through the agonies of modern Korean history. He always refused to take himself seriously, and many of his poems reflect his conviction that, as Saint Paul wrote: 'Where sin abounds, grace abounds the more.' (Rom. 5:20) He therefore liked to admit his own human weaknesses in order to stress his trust in God's mercy. At the same time, he was often heard to stress that 'without metaphysics there can be no poetry.' By metaphysics, he meant an understanding of life and the world informed by a religious dimension and at least in his own case that meant by faith in a redeeming, merciful God.

His poetry was from early on marked by a rejection of the refined symbolism and artificial rhetoric that characterized the often more highly esteemed work of senior Korean poets. Instead, Ku Sang often begins his poems with the spontaneous, artless evocation of a sudden moment of perception, in the midst of the city or of nature, and moves from there to more general considerations, frequently turning into a meditation on the presence of Eternity in the midst of very ordinary experiences. Many poems are hymns celebrating the wonder of being alive. His finest work has a Zen-style lightness and freedom and the volume *Yuchichallan* 'Infant Splendor' of 1991 combined delightfully spontaneous poems by Ku Sang with paintings by the Buddhist 'Mad Monk' Junggwang. One of the main translators of his work once wrote: 'No other Korean poet has so perfectly brought together the Christian belief that all is redeemed in God's eternity with the Buddhist conviction that all that exists is united in an unending cosmic process.' The Korean PEN Center several times proposed him for the Nobel Prize in Literature.

He was remarkable for his laughing responses to life, even in its most serious moments. He notoriously laughed while he was speaking at his wife's funeral Mass, and several of his friends remarked that it was only suitable that the photograph carried before his coffin at his funeral showed him smiling rather mischievously. In Ku Sang, Korea produced a major poet of great originality and utter personal integrity. The major French poet and critic René Tavernier once wrote of his work: 'A poetry born out of faith in God, and at the same time emerging from history, the thoughts of Ku Sang are based on experience as well as on belief: physical reality, appearances are by no means insignificant but beyond them there is another truth of which we only detect traces here and there. The thinker, the theologian, the believer are able to sense the existence of that higher universe. For Ku Sang, poetry is the sign of an inner experience.'

He wrote in the preface to *Yuchichallan* 'Infant Splendor': 'The mind of childlike innocence that we try to portray in our poems and paintings is not that state naturally found in the child before it reaches the age of discretion, but rather the condition of someone who has reached purity of heart by achieving mastery over self. Not, of course, that we claim to have attained such a state; I would rather say that we have simply been striving to fathom what might be the nature of such a state. At a time when the whole world seems fascinated by strategic values such as ownership and profit, in the midst of all this uproar, the fact is that we are eager to achieve such an innocence in our lives. While we were bringing out our series of poems and paintings, we were criticized on the one hand for being 'unrealistic,' on the other for being 'unartistic'. But since neither of us has ever had any thought of becoming the 'ornament of the age' as poet or artist, it seems not to matter!'

That recalls one of the poems from that volume, in which he tells how delighted he was to hear a neighborhood child say she had told her school teacher that she knew a famous poet 'who looks just like a little boy playing by himself.' Authenticity in him meant lightness and truth; he was never ashamed to evoke moments of sexual or other transgression, to the great surprise of many Catholic priests who wanted Korea's leading Catholic poet to present a mask of feigned respectability to the world. He is one of the very few poets to report having had a 'wet dream' in the course of a poem, and more than once recalls spending the night with a prostitute.

Ku Sang's wife died in 1994, and his two sons also predeceased him. He leaves a daughter, Ku Ja-myeong, who only a few weeks after his death received the 2004 Catholic Literary Award. At his funeral, the presence of several people in wheelchairs reminded those present of Ku Sang's constant concern for the handicapped, expressed in a number of extremely generous donations in recent years. Also, a few years ago he gave his very important library to the town of Waegwan and in 2002 a magnificent building housing it was inaugurated. But Ku Sang was already too sick to attend the ceremony.

Translations of Ku Sang's poetry began to be published when he was already over 70 and four volumes in English were published, as well as volumes in French, German, Italian, Dutch and Japanese.

# Mystery of Meeting

# A Pebble

On the path before my house
every day I meet a pebble
that once was kicked by my passing toe.

At first we just casually
brushed past each other, morning and night,
but gradually the stone began to address me
and furtively reach out a hand,
so that we grew close, like friends.

And now each morning the stone,
blooming inwardly with flowers of Grace,
gives me its blessing,
and even late at night
it waits watchfully to greet me.

Sometimes, flying as on angels' wings
it visits me in my room
and explains to me the Mystery of Meeting,
reveals the immortal nature of Relationship.

So now, whenever I meet the stone,
I am so uncivilized and insecure
that I can only feel ashamed.

# Gomo Station, Mother' s Station

Whenever I pass Gomo Station,
my mother is waiting.
Out in front of the garden gate, she is waiting,
looking scarcely older than my wife looks now,
looking just as when she saw me off
the day I crossed the 38th Parallel,
out in the lane, she is waiting.

Living helter-skelter, day by day,
rattling the empty lunch-box in my satchel,
coming home from school by train, as in that childhood,
so now when my hair is as grey
as my father's was when he died,
out by the station she is waiting.

My mother, who stayed behind
alone in our North Korean home,
alive still, or dead, I do not know,
has come here now and is waiting.

∗Note: Gomo is on the outskirts of Daegu, South Korea, and its name means 'Mother-caring, Mother-recollecting'.

# Touching Sights

Touched by an autumn afternoon's pale sunlight,
on the piano keyboard lid
lies a pair of stockings.

They must have been laid aside
by my daughter who is living abroad
when she was leaving this morning.

Seeing this still-life composition, so strange
yet so completely familiar,
after fumbling and groping in my memories:

In Daegu, down a narrow lane behind the herb market,
opening my eyes in a singing-girl's room one morning
and, laid on a chest beside my pillow,
two stocking slippers come to mind.

At the same moment I begin to murmur
a phrase from a poem by O Il-Do:
'On a tree's bare branch her basket hangs,
where then has my darling gone?'

# Mysterious Wealth

Feeling today like the Prodigal Son
just arrived back in his father's arms,
I observe the world and all it contains.

June's milky sky glimpsed through a window,
the sunlight dancing over fresh green leaves,
clusters of sparrows that scatter, chirping,
full-blown petunias in pots on verandas,
all strike me as infinitely new,
astonishing and miraculous.

My grandchild, too, rushing round the living-room
and chattering away for all she's worth,
my wife, with her glasses on,
embroidering a pillow-case,
and the neighbors, each with their particularities,
coming and going in the lane below,
all are extremely lovable,
most trustworthy, significant.

Oh, mysterious, immeasurable wealth!
Not to be compared with storeroom riches!
Truly, all that belongs to my Father in Heaven,
all, all is mine!

# Spring Chrysanthemums

At the window of a large room,
in an old orange-box
with a scrap of soil
and a packet of seeds sprinkled,
spring chrysanthemums
yellow,
red,
pink,
turquoise,
white,
are spreading their petals.

Single blossoming sign of Nature
in an artificial world!

Scarcely arrived, the spring-morning sunshine
dazzles, then slips away.

At the third floor opposite, a pink blanket
waves like a tongue while the owner,
a dancer, squints across;

above, on the sixth floor, a student is listening to jazz,
brushing the dandruff from bushy hair
and staring down.

On the ground floor a bank-guard's wife,
her perm in a towel
as she fiercely beats cushions,
pauses to glance up.

And the unmarried pensioner next door,
changing the water in his goldfish-bowl,
stops and looks sideways

while the two kid brothers to the left
stop playing at housekeeping
and turn to look.

In the street a bean-curd seller,
ringing a hand-bell as he passes,
stops and looks up

and the ice-cream man,
pushing his cart along,
looks up too, wiping his brow
while the newly-married housewife
watering her flowers
cannot help thinking of her husband
whom she has just pushed off to work,
after a good number of tongue-bites,
and very slightly she smiles.

# Knots 8.

In the coffee-shop Etranger
was Yumi,
a eurasian girl
with White Russian blood.

At first I pestered her
to become my little sister,
but with no success.

One evening, near midnight,
after several glasses of vodka,
when I suddenly fell on her cherry lips,
just that once she exclaimed,
'No acting like that, brother!'

The course of my love:
constantly such falsehoods,
no unity!
And a miserable conclusion.

Thirty years later, even now,
in the Shangri-la of dreams
I always feel anxious
about my encounter with Yumi.

Impotence of affection in me!

# Knots 9.

On my thickly growing branches
the *Duino Elegies* and the *Lotus Sutra*
brought out buds of pantheism.

My human life: a morning dewfall on grass.
All things existing,
that had hitherto been mere appearance,
were bringing forth light from within
and, day by day, dying.

One day, as the tears
of impermanence were brimming full,
a fountain of song
began to rise within me.

'Until the day when my flesh becomes leaves,
my bones stalks,
and when from my scarlet blood
a bouquet of flowers shall rise,
ah, life!'

That was the first phrase of my first poem.

# Knots 23.

*Ung-ae*
*Ung-ae*
*Ung-ae*

A new life
squirming, uttering
a newborn squalling.

Shy caresses for such an innocent being,
shared vows of fervent self-sacrifice, here crystallized,
before this new star that we two have brought rising
above the earth.

My wife, barely thirty and now a mother,
feeds the baby at her breast with a smile like a full moon
while she croons a lullaby
that I heard from my mother when I was little.

As I left her bedside,
wilting like a wild chrysanthemum,
the birth of this first child
was to me like a tonic full of new vigor.

# Knots 31.

'Do you have any idea of what our little Oki has been saying since you left?'
'Hmm?'
'That the Communists should leave Daegu alone, sail down to the sea off Busan and fire their guns there; that's what she says.'
'Hmm?'
'Because then our Mr. Ku would come right back to Daegu.'
'What's that? Even if it means the collapse of the country?'
'That girl so wants to see you, she says she doesn't care if the country collapses or not.'

Returning after carrying official messages to Busan, I called in at my usual bar and was greeted by the hostess with those words before I had even had time to sit down. At that, Oki blushed deeply and started scolding her to make her shut up.

I had been a virgin when I married and had never known any woman other than my wife but that evening I removed the Holy Medal I usually wore on my breast and laid it under the pillow before embracing that same girl, who was chattering like a fool. Even I was taken aback by my desire.

# Knots 39.

In a trench on a hill near the battle front during a pause in the fighting, our off-duty soldiers with a few black GIs were enjoying a *makkeolli* party.

They were quite far gone in drink, and it was a riot of jumbled half-words: ‘drink’ ‘ok’ ‘thank-you’ while one of the black soldiers had his arm around one of ours and was quietly chattering away to him about something eagerly, until at last he grabbed another of his companions by the scruff of the neck and pulled him near:

— Hey, student, come here and translate what this *kkamtungi* fellow is trying to tell me. He obviously wants to say something good.

— Why, he’s drunk too; he’s just making noises; it’s not worth bothering about.

But turning to the black soldier, he said:

— You say once more.

— You know, we differ in nationality, race, homeland, parents, and skin and everything. You know, we differ in many respects.

— Go ahead.

— But we are one, because we are the same — privates destined to die on the same day. We’re the same; we’re closest friends, you know. We’re number one friends. Sure true brothers.

— You are right. I know what you mean.

He stood up and clapped his hands.

— Hey, everyone! Shut up for a while. This *kkamtungi* fellow here has just said something wonderful.

One soldier shouted: ‘You idiot! Who cares what a *kkamtungi* says. Why don’t you sing something? Or dance?’

— Shut up and listen! He said: 'You and I, we're different in every way but in one respect we're the same — we're all privates and destined to die the same day.'
Everyone agreed: 'He's right, he's right. That's better than 'all one against the Communists'.'
— He means that although we're different, how could we be more closely related, because we'll die together.
Again, general agreement: 'That's even better than what the Bible says.'
— That means we're brother for life, destined to die together! Closer to one another than to parents, brothers, lovers! Right, let's drink to this tremendous fact!'
'You're better than the star Kim Dong-won playing Hamlet!'
At which our privates laughed all together, the black soldiers laughed in imitation, the party grew rowdy again, and soon the trench was echoing to a joint chorus of 'Happy Birthday to You.'

*

The allied forces go crawling upward.
There are black private soldiers among them.
Penetrating the hail of shells and bullets
one of our private soldiers reaches the top
and hurls a grenade.
A black soldier follows him up
and hurls a grenade.
Red heat, explosion after explosion, hand-to-hand . . .
As day breaks, at the summit
the South Korean flag is waving ghostlike.
The corpses of allies and foes lie side by side.
The name-tag fallen from the neck of one black soldier
glistens exceptionally bright in the morning sunlight.

# To the Students Killed on April 19, 1960

Depart in peace, brotherly souls,
without bloody complaints,
like clouds floating carelessly hand in hand
through the springtime sky.

Over fields of mugwort where gales rage,
waves of anger wringing every heart,
along the narrow way these brother have opened,
funeral corteges of freedom follow one another.

Seeds of life scattered by you our brothers!
It is not our task to cultivate and bring them to bloom
so let go of that hope, thicker than fate,
and quickly spread wings of eternal repose.

# Knots 71.

After vain efforts to decipher
this message, a single page
that fluttered down from somewhere, I have returned.

In the shade of palm trees at Kumong Pass,
beside the sea at Vongtau,
even sitting with aodai-clad bargirls
in Saigon,
I strove to decipher it, in vain;
I have returned.

It might be a propaganda leaflet
dropped by the Vietcong. I am not sure.

Or a trick by a Vietnamese boy
I met at Natrang orphanage. I am not sure.

Maybe it is a ploy of some secret service,
to test my way of thinking. I am not sure.

It might be a poster
of the Pope's appeal for peace. I am not sure.

Or perhaps, rather, it may be a last will and testament
left by one of our Korean heroes. I am not sure.

You see, it was
in the form of a falling tear.

You see, it was

in the form of prison fetters.

You see, it was
in the form of a hole
pierced by a falling shell.

You see, it was
in the form of a limbless skeleton.

Or rather, it was
in the shape of a bitter spirit unable to find rest.

Yet it seemed
to be something to do with Vietnam.

Yet it also seemed
to be something concerning me in particular.

Yet it also seemed
to concern my fellow-countrymen.

But it seemed mainly
to be a strong suggestion
aimed at all the peoples of the world.

And the only thing that I have felt
thanks to it
is that I as an individual,
that indeed the whole of humanity,
we are all still utterly ignorant. Only that.

So now, still unable
to really decipher the message,
since I have managed to return,

I publish it like this.

On a sheet of white paper
traced in red blood
a question-mark:
?
What can it mean?

# Knots 92.

After my wife's body had been brought to the funeral parlor
I was sitting idly
in a corner of the rush mat in the reception room.

After some time an employee came in;
my daughter-in-law consulted in whispers with my daughter, aunt,
then approached me.

Shrouds came priced between five hundred thousand Won
and, the most expensive, a million two hundred thousand;
they'd chosen one at six fifty thousand, but
'Father, what do you think?'

In normal times I would have replied in a flash:
'Do what you think is best,' but
catching a glimpse of my wife's portrait on the altar
I saw she was wearing, not Korean or western dress but her doctor's white coat.

I suddenly thought to myself:
I never once in her life bought her a dress.

'That one, a million two hundred thousand Won,
use one of those.'

I spat out the words like someone angry
then turned aside.

Then on further reflection I reckon

it's just as well my wife's gone to her rest because
I reckon she'd be none too pleased with such ridiculous extravagance
and after all, if she were to come alive again
I don't suppose I would pay even two hundred thousand Won
so my heart was feeling very far from well.

# Before a War Cemetery of North Korean Dead

Ah, surely they could never close your eyes,
you, souls now resting here in rows?

It was these our hands, that until yesterday
pressed the trigger and took your lives,
that gathered up your broken, rotting bodies, your bones,
then chose a secluded mountainside where the sun is right,
and quietly buried them, even covered the spot with turf,
for truly death is more mysterious
than hatred or love.

Not far from here the road is blocked,
the homeward road your souls, like mine, must take,
and the mere silence of the empty, desert hills
weighs on my breast a thousand tons;
so while in life we were only united in hate,
now rather the tragic longing
you were not able to allay
dwells within my aspiration.

In the spring sky, nearly close enough to touch,
a cloud indifferently
floats northward;
gunfire echoes from afar
and before these tombs of love and hate
all I can do is weep copious tears.

# River 36.

This yearning, this longing
which I here send adrift like
paper boats down the river
will somewhere find meeting
some day fulfillment will come.

Out in the heart of that boundless sea
up in the vastness of that stretching sky
or set reborn on this earth again
or within the divine Mystery, who knows?

But once become an immutable form
within the eternal Garden of Life

this yearning, this longing
which I here send adrift like
paper boats down the river
will somewhere find meeting
some day fulfillment will come.

# River 40.

There is a place in Wonsan Bay where a river flowing down from far inland enters the East Sea, and it is a cursed spot, where the sand is never smooth and the currents swirl strongly, that every year claims several lives. Yet it was also a fine place to wash off our naked bodies, salty from bathing and covered in sand.

One day they held an exorcism there, beside the river's mouth. The Shaman used a chicken to represent the lingering soul of someone who had fallen into the water and drowned; she flapped around in the water, screaming wildly as if possessed and giving a laudable imitation of someone drowning, then when the ceremony was over she went off, leaving the chicken lying there at the water's edge.

Among our class of Minor Seminarians, the most good-natured and most mischievous boy, one Simon, having checked that the other onlookers had gone off, picked up that chicken, borrowed a pot from an isolated house there on the shore, boiled it, then put it ready and said, 'This is the flesh of an evil spirit, so let only those who are going to become saints eat it; those who cannot become saints must not eat it, so go ahead as you think best.' The class was a little horrified at these words, but yielding to a healthy appetite that was gnawing inside, all took part in that feast of saints so that in no time at all the spirit's legs and breast were all devoured.

So those happy days went by, until one day just two or three days before term began. We had spent that whole day too by the sea and now it was time to go, so we went to wash in the fresh water of the stream. Simon, who was a step ahead of us and already in the water suddenly cried, 'I'm falling, I'm falling!' He was smiling happily -- I remember this quite

clearly -- gazing at him, I said ‘Another joke!’ and went on drying myself, but he dipped his head in the water a couple times, like someone swimming, and then he was gone!
At that I screamed, while some fishermen who had been working on the hull of their boat nearby were up in a flash, looked stunned for a moment, then went to the rescue, but it was no use and his body was taken from the water five hours later, at midnight.

That was my first direct experience of death, so there was not only fear but also a feeling of guilt at having just looked on while my friend was dying, and for a while I could not bring myself to show my face in the village. In addition there was the secret of the Shaman’s chicken added to my own insecurity, so that I said nothing to anyone, to the very end.

# River 59.

Bright as the monstrance at Vespers,
the sun shone down on the morning river, and from midstream
suddenly, walking across the water,
lo and behold, my master, St Christopher!

Coming up like some powerful spirit
to where I stood confused with surprise and joy,
he called out a question, like a Zen master:

'Brother John! It's been several years
since you chose this river for your place of work;
what have you seen in the river?'

'I have seen mystery.'
Unexpected, that was my reply.

'Brother John! It's been several years
since you chose this river for your place of work;
what have you learned from the river?'

'I have learned mystery,'
I blindly replied.

'Brother John! It's been several years
since you chose this river for your place of work;
what have you discovered from the river?'

'I have discovered mystery,' I replied,
considering the repeated questions to be a sign
of the rightness of my answer, and swelling with pride.

But the next moment my teacher,
making as if to wield the magic staff he was clutching,
glared furiously and thundered:

'You thief! You fraud! Doesn't that mean
you haven't seen anything, haven't learned anything,
haven't discovered anything?'

My head bowed with fear,
'Yes'
was all I could reply.

'Yes?! That sound is salvation, that alone.
Begin again with the river, untiringly!'

'Yes'

After a while, I lifted my head,
St Christopher was gone,
and the river was flowing on, untiringly.

# A Wry Smile

I went into Deoksu Palace gardens
on my way to give a lecture for housewives
and there, sitting on a bench in the shade
of the wisteria-covered pergola, was
my sworn friend but, would you believe it!
Well! Sitting there as bold as could be
elbow to elbow with some young thing!

I simply couldn't believe it of him,
so I called out, 'Old fellow!' to embarrass him
and he came across, saying,
'Are you jealous or something?'

'Do as well as you can!
I'm for the flower-beds too!'
a bantering reply
but going on my way I reflected:
he's over seventy
and his wife died last year
he's living alone in the flat
so maybe.... I thought.

When I came out after giving my talk
there was my friend sitting downcast
alone on the bench
— Jilted already?
I asked mockingly.
— My granddaughter, fallen in love,
ran away from home, wanted to talk,
he replied, smiling wryly.

I likewise gave a wry smile and together
we strolled off towards our usual bar.

# Playing by Himself

Before the little girl next door
went to primary school
one day on seeing me she said,
'Granddad, they say you're famous?'
So I asked her,
'What's famous?'
She replied,
'I don't know!'
and I told her,
'It's something not good!'

This year, now in the second grade of middle school,
she studied one of my poems printed in their text-book,
and told me she had said that she knew the poet well.
'So what did you tell them?'
I asked;
'That you're just an ordinary old man, but
that you look like a little boy playing by himself!'
she replied.

I was delighted with her answer:
'Well done! Thank you!'
I said, praising her,
and felt cheerful for the rest of the day.

# A Bed of Roses

I am glad and grateful and happy.

Wherever one is, that is the best place to be.

Maybe you think that where you are now is a bed of thorns,
but you see, really it's
a bed of roses, the best place to be!

I am glad and grateful and happy.

# River

# Christopher's River: Prologue

Christopher!
Like you, I have chosen the river
as a place for conversions of heart.

But still, to hoist people up
onto my back, as you did,
and carry them over the water,
or to make a simple boat
and row them across,
why, I have neither the strength nor the skill;

and to do things for people, like you,
with a pure heart,
I admit I possess neither aim nor resolve.

Besides, even when I am out by the river, I find
no way to renounce the whole world, as you did;
I am so caught in the cords of normality
that as they are tugged, like a puppet I turn
round and round, round and round.

Christopher!
As I am, I follow you
out to the river.

And I hope and believe that if I go,
though only mimicking your simple self-discipline,
then, as at the weary end of a certain day you
met long-awaited Love's Incarnation,
so my poetry too may see the light of salvation:

in that hope and belief
I follow you out to the river.

# River 1.

Fog
lies thick
over the morning river,

Sailing, it seems, to the world beyond,
a ferryboat glides away
wrapped in vast whiteness.

In a poplar's branches up on the bank,
one solitary magpie flaps
noisily.

The submerged sand
shines bright
like a woman's secret flesh.

Swarms of tiny fish
full of inborn joy
drift by.

Golden sunbeams striking down
create a garden, a dream.

And I too, in the midst of all this, am
surely no mere rice-eating brute.

# River 2.

The hills, wrapped in monks' sombre robes,
draw near, settle down.

The silence of a shrine flows round.

The grass-green river waters
flushed with a ruddy glow,
are patterned with silver, with gold,
then become a snowy waste,
then put on a black veil.

The village across the river
like an altar
sends up incense smoke

and from a jetty,
in a fragile bark lit by a lantern
a lonely soul sets out.

# River 5.

Wind rises on the river.
Dark green ripples
furrow the surface,
sending waves slapping
onto the sandy shore.

Can it be that the river too bears
a grievance it cannot express?
It chatters as if complaining
and makes such a fuss.

The sky disgorges inky clouds,
and the wind is entangled in linen shrouds.

From off the pale cowering sands
clusters of jackdaws fly up and away
over hills wrapped in a misty rain.

# River 9.

Watching how the river waters flow
around red mountain slopes,
I bring to mind that moment when
a single drop of dew, long seeping
through the crust of earth, sprang out,
a tiny spring high up there on a desolate peak.

Watching how the river waters wind
across the verdant fields,
I picture when at last they reach
their destined ocean's waiting vastness
and flowing into the billowing waves
leap beyond the bounds of time.

Watching how the river waters flow
with perfect ease before me,
I imagine when at last
this river, now all transmigration
with its repeated evaporations,
and I, the carcass of Karma-destiny then thrown off,
will meet again upon this spot as living beings.

# River 10.

Laid along the valleys here and there,
having cast off their carcass of flesh and blood,
nothing but a handful of earth,
here now the ancient dead flow by.

Thus the river clasps to its breast
the desires and sorrows of every person
and flows.

So one day, soon, as I flow by,
shall I not encounter
the unthinking gaze of my youngest child
now fishing here,
of his son or grandson at least?

And then one day,
all turned to praise,
I shall sit here again myself!

# River 11.

It was merely water.
It was a great mass of water.
That great mass of water
flowed indifferent on.

Flowing on, it always
stayed in that same place.
Staying in that same place,
it was constantly renewed.

Renewed, although the past
continued steadfast there.
The past continued steadfast,
but the future too was there.

Past and future, thus united,
became one single present.
And that single present moment
showed many faces there.

It showed so many faces,
spoke in many voices.
Speaking many voices,
its heart was indifferent to all.

Always to all indifferent, it suffered,
and suffering it was still indifferent.
Indifferent, one day it died
and dying returned to life.

# River 16.

The river
continues the past,
is not imprisoned by the past.

The river,
while living today
lives the future too.

The river,
though innumerably collective,
keeps unity and equality.

The river
makes itself an empty mirror
in which all things view themselves.

The river
at all times and in all places
chooses the lowest place.

The river,
unresisting, accepts
every violence, every humiliation,
and never denies itself.

The river
gives freely to all that lives
and looks for nothing in return.

The river

is its own master,
free despite all bonds.

The river,
caught between generation and extinction,
reveals Eternity within impermanence.

The river
every day in its Pantomime
teaches me many things.

# River 18.

Beneath the river bed
that our human eyes can see
there flows another river,
deep and wide.

Piercing downwards and sideways,
forming eyes for the lace-like strata,
sparkling like the dawn
in the deepest darkness,
it flows.

And down that silver river
petrified beasts and plants
float like sailing ships,
with at times a human corpse.

And all around those dead things,
like a thick mist, float
those dreams
and loves
and tears
and grudges
and prayers
that alive they kept within.

My poetic thoughts are there too,
the things I can neither express nor represent.

# River 20.

I have spent today,
that source of mystery, today,
wallowing in the dirt.

Along the sewers of my soul,
so full of stench and running muck,
the spirits of all purity
have foamed and died.

Tomb of Time turned to a muddy slough!
Just a trickle of tears flows from the drain
and drips into the coal-black stream.

Sun and moon, and time too, have lost their shine,
and all those things that once bloomed flowers of grace
reciprocate now with a wilting look.

Ah! When will that day come
when my life and all its meaning
will flow into the distant sea
and recover eternal freshness?

# River 35.

Young springtime sunlight gleams
with a sparkle of silver fish leaping
from the early-morning river
as white water-fowl fly up like
baby angels.

A shaggy-faced hill
shakes off slumber
and approaches the river's brink
while from the tip of an accompanying poplar
a single magpie cackles.

In the village, plum-blossomed like a victory shout,
from chimneys perched on toy-like thatched cottages
the morning smoke rises like incense,

from the barley-fields a breath of green comes wafting
like the scent of fresh chicken droppings

and as I wash my coal-black heart
in this child-fresh river
it conjures up rainbow dreams.

# Christopher's River: Epilogue

The river flows...

as the bier carries off the days long past,
and the procession is filled with things yet to come,
so, bearing all the vast emptiness of a long, remote story,

the river flows...

bearing the mysterious wonder of the birth
of a tear-like dewdrop that has passed through the earth,
from a secret source like a virgin's fountain

the river flows...

murmuring all its mottled yearning,
touching the wounds received in falling
against the rocky sides of bottomless chasms,
slipping through the stony labyrinths of knowledge,

the river flows...

tingeing with hope and shame
all the passionate romanticism of the world's vast plains,
the solitude and prayer that arise in marshes,
and, ah, the bitter memories of wandering and chill,

the river flows...

now beneath Time's indifferent stare,

bearing in its breast the playfulness of water creatures,
on its back craft of painful labor and of pleasure,
gliding below bridges where good and evil, love and hatred pass,
hearing whispers of love and songs of parting,
groans of birth, groans of death, the grief of bitter souls,
making symphony with the rhythms of all that lives,

the river flows...

in sources and rapids, falls and streams,
all the hosts of being join, mingle, unite,
begetting, dying, flowing into the azure sea
to become the origin of new generation
until history at last, in sinuous fullness, perfectly ends,

the river flows...

without any shadow of past or future,
with a constant identity in a world of change,
with a love more solid than any rock,
breathing each present moment in Eternity,

the river flows...

with no concern about imminent evaporation,
weeping with desire for non-being,
smiling at the flower of illusion,

the river flows...

River! Essence of the unbeing Void!

# Fields

# Here and There

A turnip field on a mountainside.
Around an ancient, springtime-drowsy rock
a single blowfly buzzes.

It comes and goes, all the time,
among old, panlid-like pats of dung
that lie in the grass on the crestward path,
now perching low on the rock's shaded waist,
now squatting high on its sunburned brow,
now moistening itself at the stagnant water
held in deep pits on its rocky crown,

then delicately folding its legs in prayer,
depositing spots of pustular waste
or laying tiny, nit-like eggs,

then flying off to land on a spring chrysanthemum's stamens,
a single red spot in the midst of the turnip field,
and there, like a little boy hypnotized by a cinema screen,
staring down at fields, rivers, roads,
as they stretch out level to the far horizon
and suddenly the world seems all suspended,
like a green, dead body,
a moment without the sound of breathing,
a moment delivered from starvation, disdain and slaughter,
this moment, without curses or conspiring,

and somehow, blowfly, dungfly,
as if for you this stillness
bred a grieving fear,

echoing, your buzzing seems to weep.

# Within Creation

Beneath the garden fence,
all round the storage platform,
the rose moss blooms.

With multi-colored stamens
crowning the soft white stems
they flirt there, posing,
nudging and jostling,
rubbing their cheeks, they bloom.

The water-melon moon
is perched high in the sky;
the night, nearly spent, is moist with dew,
and tiny butterflies come visiting,
no larger than the brooch
on my younger daughter's breast,
they hover lightly over the stamens,

yellow,
red,
pink,
green,
violet,
purple,

these butterflies, flitting from stamen to stamen
in pollen quest!
Swarms of butterflies, since spring began,
even by night, flying innumerable!

Thus bringing colors to the rainbow flowers
over thousands of years, how huge a task
these tiny things have performed, to be sure!

Behind the shed soft persimmons hang red
which, before autumn came,
would scorch and shrivel your mouth;
on the hill above, the chestnuts, too,
having bristled with spines to keep strangers at bay,
now that the nuts are ripe
and shine ready to fall,
open their mouths of their own accord.

Ah, every creature, every one,
knows the meaning of here, and tomorrow,
and so they live in togetherness,
assisting each other with all their hearts;
so how is it that I, a man, stand here
this night, all alone, like a rotting stick in a fence,
understanding nothing?

# Springtime Dances

The old plum tree stump,
wimpled in white,
is dancing the dance of the crane.

The towering pine trees,
extending green parasols in either hand,
are performing a waltz.

Weeping willows sway in rhythms free,
bony acacias
rock leafless shoulders,
while bamboos rubbing arms and legs
step it out together.

Along the wayside where snow meets the sun
tiny blades of grass, already sprouting,
gently sway.

Seeds, roots, insects, frogs,
that had only been peeping from underground windows
now put on their springtime best,
like actors in backstage dressing rooms.

Now the breath of spring in the breeze
comes gently brushing the naked flesh.

# Spring Washing

Along the edge of a barley field
weeping willow trees
dip their tresses in a stream.

Sunbeams beneath the water,
turned to golden grains of sand, dance
then pause, then flow again.

Hunched like toads
new crawled from the ground,
the village women and girls
attack the springtime washing.

Slip-slop. slip-slop,
tacka-tacka-tacka, slosh-slosh,
they beat away
as if pounding out the rice-cake paste.

Chick-check, chick-chock,
yick-yeck, yick-yock,
heh-heh, hee-hee! The tongues wag away:

Here's a baby girl born in the year of the horse!
The father-in-law's not too pleased about that!
And here's a mother-in-law too strict by half,
or a cheeky student for a sister-in-law,
but there a husband's gone back after leave,
and as for the gangsters of a certain political party...

In this pleasant scene

there still remain shadows of personal pain,
like stains in the embroideries
made by young widows.

# Moonlit Evening

As the moon was bathing lazily
in the still waters of a well,
she was caught in the bucket, up she went,
was poured out into a stoneware jar.

Scooped from there in a fresh hollow gourd,
she flowed all down a bride's black hair,
over creamy back and swelling breasts,
down she slipped, and away she went,
splashing into shivers on a washing-stone.

The moon-washed flesh was now white as moon...

From high up on the straw-pale roof
the pepper-pods look down,
their faces blush redder than ever.

Glancing up at the moon,
now somehow back up on high,
the pumpkins are embarrassed
and shyly creep under their vines.

In the flower-beds the balsam flowers watch it all,
they see and drop petals at so much fun,
moistening their eyes with dewdrops.

# Garden by Moonlight

In the garden beneath the new moon
faces of times gone by return.

That face peeping out from the balsam flowers?
A cousin who, three days after her wedding,
left for the North;
giving me a set of colored thimbles,
she left, with a hoarse whistle cry from the train,
but that same face, rosy as fifty years ago,
is slyly peeping out at me now.

In the cosmos flowers, the catechism sister!
Agnes, was it? Or Lucy?
With black wimple and white veil
framing her face, that ivory sister,
object of my tiny heart's deep longing,
that tall, tall foreign sister
is smiling out at me now.

And that face among the chrysanthemums,
whose might that be?

It looks like the dead face of my mother,
laid somewhere unknown in the North,
or my sister-in-law's gentle face,
(she too stayed behind),
but it could also be my future daughter-in-law's.

The crescent moon slips behind an inky cloud,
the garden now seems dizzy,

frightened too, maybe,
and wrapped in an icy breath.

Could I be developing a chill?

# Fields 2.

Urging on his ox,
a farmer ploughs his field.

The long-blocked pores of the ground
burst open once more.

The frozen lungs
expand again.

The spring sky seems
almost near enough to touch.

Ox and peasant
glance upwards together.

A cloud slowly drifts
North-wards.

Moooo!

The ploughshare bites into the ground
and rips its way through
thorns and creepers.

# Fields 3.

Just three days married!
Stealing sly glances at each other,
a young couple treads down the barley field
which, still frozen, creaks beneath their feet.

Patching up the rutted rice-field banks with soil,
as if firming up their swelling, restless hearts,
step by step they tread down the ground.

To the East outpouring sunbeams break through,
to the South a haze dances over the hills
like a nylon veil;
on the branches of an old West-leaning tree
yellow and red jackets blossom,
bearing waterpots on their heads;
in the village that lies to the North
the sweet smoke of morning smoothly rises
from chimneys over yellow thatch.

Like motes of dust in a hothouse,
swarms of gnats dance before my eyes,
the birds flutter, dive and chirp.

A smell like chicken droppings
drifts across from somewhere.

In the morning when the ground first thaws
the whole world exhales beauty.

# Fields 4.

Young Dog-shit's granddad,
in his dog-shit-rich fields
has emptied out shit from a basket of cane
and is spreading it round.

Millet pancakes: cow shit,
flower-shaped rice-cakes: horse shit,
coal-dust ovoids: pig shit,
raw oysters: chicken shit,
black beans: rabbit shit,
black flower-seeds: rat shit,
goat shit, donkey shit, fox shit,
shit, just call it shit,
lies scattered over the field.

Young Dog-shit saunters out,
with fish-guts hanging
from his snuffling nose,
he pulls down his dreadful ash-coloured pants,
spotted and coated with remains of rice,
and revealing his azalea-pink behind,
he strains and groans to deposit a turd.

Little Brownie comes out after him,
and goes snuffling with his shiny nose
around the furrows of the field
with their clusters of dung in crusts and scabs,
releasing a trickle of urine
before at last he expells a hard one, hiss,
and comes rushing across, wagging his tail,

trying to lick his master's behind.

Young Dog-shit raises his arse-hole aloft,
then grasping a long stick still steaming
he has plunged into the dung-pit
he drives him off, you cur, you cur,
waving the stick between his legs.

Then, lifting up his drooping head,
as he gazes at the bluish waning moon
still hanging on a northward fence
he conjures up a picture of those wild melons,
last year in summer, with their taste of honey,
but that brings back memories
of thundering stomach-ache and cramping diarrhoea
so that he shakes his head from side to side.

This time I must only eat one, or two, or three,
no more, he mutters, as with his stick-clutching hand
he presses down fingers on his left hand,
one by one counting off two whole fingers.

Up on the little hill over opposite, see
that wild apricot breaking into blossom like a battle-cry!
Skipping up and down from branch to branch,
one solitary magpie,
ejecting droppings like white grubs,
cackles to itself in pleasure.

# Fields 17.

Hey, you!
Are you big?
See, I'm bigger!

Hey, there,
look and see
which is redder?

It's ripe
so eat.
yum yum yum.

One corner
of the nursery-school garden
is a field of paprika plants.

# Fields 26.

Just as many people, busy memorizing one by one
the names of mythological Greek divinities,
names you can't get your tongue around,

seem not to know of Master Baek-kyeol, or Lady Suro,
of Master Sosan, or Lady Sa-Imdang,

and just as so many young girls,
expert in the loves of Cleopatra,
of Romeo and Juliet, Marilyn Monroe, or BB,
or the passionate affairs of Broadway and Hollywood,

seem not to know the hard realities
of the life of their housemaids at home,

and though they enjoy tulips, cannas, gladioli,
cyclamens, hyacinths,
even changing their make-up to harmonize with them,

yet they seem to despise us, looking down their noses
as if we had no connection with their past or future,
and don't even know our names.

Think of all those traditional nicknames,
homely and piquant,
that countryside parents give to their children,
names that we love as soon as we hear them:
Rocky, Iron-stone, Rolling-stone,
Dog-shit, Cow-shit, Iron-heart,
Great Wain, Bear, Everlasting,

Beauty, Grace, Cup-Cake,
Twisty, Docile, Moon,
Powder, Blossom.

Of course, dandelion, shepherd's-purse, rocambole,
cottonweed, clover, windflower,
leopard-flower, bellflower, or nettles,
everyone knows that kind of name,

but widowers-relish, beads-in-a-purse,
clowns-beard dead-nettle, dandruff-head,
dogs-eggs-herb, fleas-nest,
frog-food duckwort,
goblins-bridle, knotted samphire, nuncle-beet,
lady's-button, ants pagoda, kiss-the-moon,
virgins lichen, thieves-by-the-way, goblins needle,
beggars vine, toddlers-grass, madman,
did you ever even hear
such delightful, natural names?

Fix flourishing stamens
like a widower's hair
to a stem in the ground,
you have widowers-relish,

fix flowery pockets to either side
of a stubby stalk
and what you have is beads-in-a-purse,

let the shape of the flower be like two purple lips,
then by attaching two wisps of beard-like stamens
to the three parts of the lower jaw
you get clowns-beard flowers,

if all the body is covered with short fur,
has short-toothed leaves,
and two reddish flowers
dingle-dangling,
no wonder you call it
dogs-eggs-herb,

leaves shaped like globes,
the whole plant covered with thinish hairs,
the flowers seem covered with fleas
so you call it fleas-nest,

still to be found exposed to the snow
on winter lily-ponds:
frog-food duckwort,

attached to a tendril,
a great leaf up to one meter long,
so polished it looks grotesque,
goblins' bridle,

beside the sea,
great knotted stalks, and fixed to each
grows knotted samphire

also by the sea,
just like a large beet
with a beard attached,
nuncle-beet,

the naked body of a pretty girl
blooming inside a flower,
lady's button,

a spike of flowers
seemingly invaded by a swarm of red ants,
since it blossoms yellow-brown:
ants pagoda,

kiss-the-moon
has soft cotton fur all over
and on summer nights its yellow flowers
open wide and look delightful

virgins' lichen
hangs in swaying threads
from Cheju Island's trees and rocks,
while the leaves and spore-pods seem swollen with eggs.

the very name of thieves-by-the-way sounds wicked
and if ever its hairy seeds get stuck to your clothes,
there is no way of getting them off again,

goblins needle too
has needle-like seeds that cling,

beggars vine
is a mess, like dirty handmarks and footprints,
toddlers-grass
oozes yellow juice,

while madman
is dark and disordered, leaves and flowers,
all seemingly dipped in muddy water.

There are others too, too many to tell;
ladies underwipe, truth-to-tell,
hat mushroom, fly-catcher, violet, sticky-spoon,

eight-fingers,
if we preserve and respect
the names and the features of each of our friends,
who knows where it may end?

From ancient days we have often heard
'Heaven won't produce a wageless man,
Earth won't grow a nameless plant'

As people declare 'No one is above another,
no one is beneath another,'
by roadside, in fields' furrows and on mountain slopes,
without asking for anyone's help,
growing up by nature, fulfilling natural duties,
then naturally passing away, see, our true life!

And even you whom men call poets
rashly call these weeds
and so reject them!

# Fields 39.

In the autumn sky
flocks of wild geese fly away.
Casting long shadows
over my aching heart,
northwards they fly.
Each seems to hold the other's tail
as in straight lines they fly away.

Flapping
    flapping
        flapping
            flapping
                flapping
                    flapping
                        flapping
                            flapping
they drop down and settle in the cavities in my breast.
                                        do
                                    re
                                mi
                            fa
                        sol
                    la
ti
the last one
I captured.

Throb
throb

throb
my heart is racing
honk
honk
honk
my heart is weeping
honk
honk
honk
the sky is weeping
honk
honk
I set it free.

That single, lonely, flying form
is like me.

In the autumn sky
flocks of wild geese fly away,
within my heart
in parallel lines they fly away.

# Fields 42.

In the snow-sprinkled morning field,
his hair likewise frosted white,
a man stood idle.

Not like someone involved in days of plenty,
weaving sweetest dreams,
he seemed to be emerging harrassed
from a hard long night of pain.

Perhaps slow to get to work
beneath accumulated disasters,
while the field, incapable of yielding a harvest,
lay there, matted dry grass, an empty abyss,
except where some greens grew
in inopportune corners,
like his innocent offspring.

Receiving the gold-bright sunshine,
the frost-hardened ground
and the man's breast too
breathed out misty bitterness

as a gust of early winter's icy wind
shook in passing the last dead leaf
on an ancient branch at the top of the field,
and in the man's eyes
drew up an icy dew.

# Sin and Grace

# Concerning the Void

My young friends!
If you wish to hear this message,
fist of all empty your hearts
and make them jars
without lid of desire
or base of anxiety.

If you do that, the rainbow of desires
and Fate with all its purulence
will be scattered wide,
like dandelion puff.
The cords of love and hate will break.
The bars of good and bad will gape.
The watch-towers of myth will crumble.
At last, I say, in peace
you will be free.

My young friends!
What is called the Void
is in fact full possession.
From darkness to light,
from fire to water,
from mud to the garden,
from food to the sewer,
from wind to the inside of the stone,
from the human to the beast,
from the fish to the worm,
from the eyes of the prisoner to the eyes of the guard,

from the queen to the beggar,

from poetry to science,
from war to peace,
flowing like melted snow
in springtime streams,
it was from the beginning
like the white spaces left
in oriental paintings,
giving birth to life and death,
to splendor and decay,
filling time and space
utterly and completely.

Therefore the Void
brings into perfect harmony
existence and generation,
as it makes possible
the co-existence of Destiny and Freedom
and, offering up the paeans of all existence,
as it brings within itself that vast celestial vault
into correspondence with itself
it is entirely a matter of mystery.

My young friends! What is this condition?
Let me assure you,
it lies in the reconciled acknowledgement
of life emerging from the blessing
of the blind abyss
and rising to the splendor of the heights.

# White Lotus

In the wastelands of my heart,
sprung up unknown to man or beast,
is one white lotus plant.

In my desert-thirsty heart,
alas, why has this bud sprung up?
For now it should bloom, but it finds no way,
this white lotus flower.

Although I anxiously watch all night,
you have no wall to shield you from harm:
suppose the urchins pluck you away?
I could only suffer, frozen, dumb.

Passers-by, coveting you,
may carry you off, root and all;
I ought to prevent that, but have no means,
bud in my heart of a white lotus flower.

If you had simply never sprung up at all,
I would not have cared, most special flower;
but now, when I see you near by or afar,
the lids of the eyes of my soul inflame.

# Impermanent I

Nowadays, in that world of other people
that flows away like Time,
my formerly panting breath subsides,
and even repentance grows faint in my breast.

As I tread on my shadow,
now more real than myself,
and stand aimlessly
like a reed waving in a dream,
and from a hole in my worn pocket
hopes and memories leak away,
fag ends and loves drop away,
bit by bit everything falls away,

no drug or drink to drown things in,
alone, awake, I stand.
Nothing matters at all.

# News of Death

This spring
news of a friend's death
came twice within three days.

The ones we love and miss go first.

A poet's income being what it is,
I avoid funerals.

Whenever I stand before someone dead
I feel it's my turn next.

But nothing at all is ready.

My life has been far too unfaithful,
I have failed my family
and the world too much.

And when I enter the other world,
I shall be ashamed to meet parents or neighbors.

And then, towards God
I feel nothing but dread.

Yet news of my death
cannot be long in coming.

# Addition to Exodus

You know, in those days too they made
a golden calf and worshipped it.

Trust, sincerity or love,
such basic necessities of existence,
thrown aside like old sticks or worn-out boots,
they became beasts,
fighting one another, simply wearing human masks.

The world, with Aaron's hoardes in charge,
became a place of submissiveness.

But even then there were people
trusting, waiting for Moses to come down from Sinai,
simply, in solitude.

Ah, Canaan,
flowing with milk and honey!
Ah, far off and how hard to reach.

# Shame

In the zoo,
peering between bars and netting,
I search for an animal
that knows what is shame.

I say, keeper!
Might there just possibly be
in those monkeys' red posteriors
at least some trace of it?

What of the bear's paw, perpetually licked?
Or the seals' whiskers,
or maybe the parrot's beak?
Is there really no trace of it there?

Since shame has vanished
from this city's people,
I came to the zoo to look for it.

# Christmas Lament

Ah, the venerable Church!
With none of the simple joy of those shepherds
who came first of all
to worship around your crib!
With nothing left of the peace of your stable.

Fearing the coming of your kingdom,
tonight too Herod and his henchmen keep watch,
ready to lop off your young shoots,
keeping Christmas with glaring eyes.

And your disciples,
changing the color of the Gospel
like a beaded dress displayed in a shop window,
the color varying with the lighting,
with the enthusiastic mob,
and the Pharisees, today too,
all crowd around
you;

and like Zaccaeus perched in a tree,
one crow-like soul cries:
'On me and on all held in cursed bondage
turn, oh turn your eyes!'

# Weeping of Magpies

On the roof of Seoul City Hall,
magpies in a cage, earlier than others
show running eyes.
Partly on account of the all-pervading exhaust fumes,
but mainly they weep
because their present life is so awful.

Pecking at the grain that is regularly scattered, they weep.
Sipping the water in a bowl, they weep.
Watching the pigeons in the square fly up and down, they weep.
Looking across to the distant hills,
seeing the trees in the near-by park, they weep.
Watching the cars lined up nose-to-tail, they weep.
Beholding the activities of the people coming and going, they weep.
Seeing the source of all authority at times appear, they weep.
Huddled at night in artificial nests, they weep.
Looking up by night at the stars in the sky, they weep.
Recalling the past, they weep.
Imagining the future, they weep.
And if they consider the chicks
that hatch and grow up in their cage,
the tears pour down.

On the roof of Seoul City Hall,
magpies in a cage, earlier than others,
show running eyes.

# The Pen

As a drop of dew penetrates the ground
then issues as a springing source,
with that same limpid energy
let us wield the pen.

As men set fire to dense forests
then till the wild and create new fields,
with that same fertile vision
let us wield the pen.

With all the arduous sweat of the miner
piercing rock a thousand feet below
let us wield the pen.

With all the precision and care
of the surgeon's scalpel in an open heart
let us wield the pen.

With reasoned thought
bright as the snow on high mountains,
with the dexterity of soldiers
checking front-line positions,
with the slave's resolve and determination
as he breaks his irons with his bare teeth,
overcoming discouragement and despair
like Sisyphus,

vested with a love
that weeps even to see
a new-sprung weed trampled on,

with the spiritual poverty of a Baek-kyeol,
let us wield the pen.

*Note: Baek-kyeol, literally 'Hundred Patches' was a famous scholar renowned for his great poverty and integrity.

# In a Winter Street

The winter twilight hangs despairingly
like the tattered banner on the red brick building,
while on the sidewalk before a crippled fence,
with strips of cement sacks in place of a sandy beach,
a few baby tortoises
lie heaped together.

The salesman stands there,
gaunt as the bare trees along the roadside,
veiled in a whitish dust,
and when his spidery hand pulls the thread it holds,
the baby tortoises scrabble, scatter,
scrabble, scrabble, scatter,
and fall off their paper shore.

Rattle, rattle, crash!
As the shutters slam down in front of the bank
a veil of darkness descends before the eyes;
a wave of people presses on, unseeing,
and with a dock-side uproar
buses screech in and away.

As the coal-black waters of a meager stream
flow unseen beneath the asphalt where he stands,
so too in the hungry innards of the salesman,
scrabble, scrabble, the turtles run
and as they run they fall.

In the lamp-light,
shining there like a lighthouse on a desert island,

the scraps of paper seem a sea-bed
viewed through a fish-eye lens,
or a tomb on which a flock
of jackdaws has settled.

In this desolate scene,
suppose the corpse of some dead wartime companion
should come up and clasp his hand,
I reckon he would weep for joy.

# Knots 1.

A bridled,
foaming,
drooling cow.

At the age of three, my first revelation of really existing
found in a face like that printed by blood and sweat on a cloth
held out by a Jerusalem woman to a man on his way to execu-
tion,
the face of a cow.

The yellow, twilit path slid up over a mountainside,
calligraphic in black and white;
and as I sat there perched on the leading cart,
in the face of the cow following behind
with an ancient chest roped to its back,
my first buds of knowledge unfolded and I wept.

# Knots 35.

Scene 1.

Down the street, urchins troop round a strangely-dressed girl. Some throw stones, other wave sticks dipped in cow pats or horse dung.
'Whore! Whoooore! Whore!'
They are set to deal with sullied motherhood according to their law.
'I'm not your mother am I? Suppose I am a whore? What of it!'
She spits out the words from foaming lips, as a passing American jeep stops, then zooms away like the wind. Only the sound of the shouts remains.

Scene 2.

A heavily made-up woman passes, in western clothes. Kids wink at one another.
One creeps up behind and skillfully fixes a sign on her back: '3000 won a trick'.
'Waha! Wahaha! Wahahaha!'
Realizing that their resistance is pointless, the children indulge in loud laughter where scorn is overlaid with self-torment.
The woman checks her heels, corrects her poise.
But until she vanishes
'Waha! Wahaha! Wahahaha!' does not abate.

Scene 3.

Gradually such pranks become rarer, and down dark alley-

ways between rough wooden shacks, children stand here and there waiting for someone.
If a drunken soldier, black or white, heaves into view, frond-like hands grab at hardened arms and tug.
'Hello! Ok? Madam, nice! Nice! Ok?'
Having had a taste of money, the children have found their own way of exploiting this wretched reality.

# Knots 79.

Now, sitting here on Dreyfus'
Bench,

I ponder the world
with the heart of the convict Jean
leaning on a palm tree
gazing into the distance after Papillon

as he sailed away
across the night sea.

I have come to realize that
keeping company with intensely dangerous
gangs of thugs in a single cell,
under the fierce stares
of the guards of 'The Island of Death'
and fulfilling my duty of raising
a herd of two hundred pigs

is neither better nor worse
than any other kind of life in this world!

I have learned that
there is no country in this world
without iron bars and chains
either visible or invisible,
and that there is only a degree of freedom that can be changed
taking our inner heart as territory
and using our various kinds of bonds as instruments!

Therefore standing here,
with no freedom or paradise
that can be attained anew,
is such a lonely thing.

*Note : In Henri Charrière's *Papillon*, the main character, known as Papillon, escapes from the French penal colony on Cayenne in French Guinea, known as 'Devil's Island' or 'the Isle of Death,' on his ninth attempt after thirteen years. He is helped by the ethnic Chinese convict Jean, who refuses to go with him. In the 19th century, the French officer Alfred Dreyfus spent many years in the same prison colony after being wrongly convicted of espionage, in a case that deeply divided French society. This poem was written in 1977, when I finally turned down a position I had been offered at Seton Hall University near New York.

# Knots 82.

Henceforth I will no longer make the hours of life turgid and foul
by vain desires,
turning the source of mystery
into a stream of coal-black sewage.

Now I have opened my eyes to the divine grace
encompassing my life,
so from henceforth as I practice Eternity
I will show forth, bear witness in myself to
the reality of the Good, the Beautiful, the True.

In days gone by I clearly saw as I went my way
the transience and failure of all possession
as I turned away from ways unseen by the eyes
esteeming and serving only visible affairs.

Again, I clearly saw as I went my way
the immortality of those who are poor in heart
who respond to the deep call of Eternity,
firmly embracing faith, hope and love.

Now I give thanks for my inabilities
and my weaknesses
and all I need for my future life
is purity of heart. Nothing else.

# Knots 98.

I have spent my whole life
deceiving myself.

This is because I have dreaded
confronting myself more than anything.

Within the heart of one part of myself
is a precipitous quicksand a thousand fathoms deep

and squirming at the bottom of it
like a villain, my heart toward which
I have lived with eyes shut or averted
like someone suffering from
acrophobia or claustrophobia.

In fact, merely in my own eyes
the conscience, humanity, morality, collaboration
I have practiced outwardly and even
the Christian life practiced as a kind of insurance

all of them, a kind of dressing up for the sake of convenience
in a life devoid of sincerity or authenticity,
drank themselves into a stupor
with that chameleon-like disguised liquor.

Besides, all my life I have claimed to be writing poetry
and absorbed myself in merely concocting sweet words
so I have lived devoted entirely to sin!

But now in a not too distant future

at the gates to the beyond, in the divine mirror
I shall have to confront the true image
of my vile, disgusting self; what shall I do!

God, let it not be so!

# Knots 100.

Today's world is veiled in thick darkness.
From here and there within that dark night
alarm signals can be heard, appealing for help.

The whole world is full of the benefits of civilization.
Drunk with freedom, systems of thought quarrel,
create an uproar like that of cicadas or frogs
but the world, like a boat with a broken compass,
is shaken, with neither center nor direction.

Meantime, shall we say that we still enjoy peace in all that?
The crowd that makes golden calves to serve,
drunk with fraud and gambling, competition and pleasure,
are spending all this dread night in debauchery.

What
can I do amidst all this?
What could a new Ten Commandments mean to such people?
No, there's no need for anything new.
But how could anyone be subject to
those ten commandments?

When things are like this, suspend all judgment!
All that remains is to entrust and pray
to the almighty, infinite Mercy.

# River 8.

Those clear spring-waters
that rose in May-time forests
now flow here, a coal-black river.

Sun and moon and clouds too
have lost their splendour,
the fresh green woods and hills
are cliffs on an ink-painted scroll.

Where the excrements of greed
issue from the sewers,
you can see, spread like a sheen of oil
over the foaming rocking water, such obscenity!

When will the day come
for our river to flow out into the blue sea?

A single flower of compassion
floats, a lotus.

# New Year

Who ever saw a new year, a new morning, all on its own?

Why! You yourself are polluting
each day, that source of mystery,
and just turning it into coal-black waste:

who ever saw a tattered day, a worn-out hour?

If you are not made new
you cannot welcome the new morning as new,
you can never welcome the new day as new;

if your heart's simplicity is once able to bloom,
then you can live the new year as new.

# Rebirth

You should not make the mistake of thinking
that the childlike heart the sages proclaim
is the state that precedes the age of discretion;

for that kind of infancy, infant immaturity,
is shackled by instinctive impulses
or else is merely complacent and narrow,

while the spirit of childhood
that we have to attain

is an innocence, a simplicity,
an artlessness
that arise from 'rebirths' such as
recognition of the truth
and victory over self.

# April

Baby buds and baby sprouts,
baby leaves and baby flowers:
hills and fields, gardens, paths,
all together blaze with green flames.

Above and below, dazzling bright.
Everything warm and snug.

Who said this is the cruellest month?
Don't attribute to the seasons
all the devastations of your heart!
Don't shut your eyes, then say it's dark.

April is Mother of Charity,
a world of new greens, and of children.

# The World of Grown-Ups

Don't mock me and say:
Why are you so sunk in thought?
It doesn't suit your little form!

The reason I am so shocked and dumbfounded
and quite at a loss for words

is, well, oh dear, well,
is the fact that
what you adults call 'life'
is so crammed full of lies.

You shout justice, yet you act unjustly,
you mouth love, yet you hate each other,
you advocate peace as you fight and kill.

I fear I am very impertinent
but as someone else has said

unless you regain the heart of a child
you cannot enter the Kingdom of Heaven and
likewise if you do not regain the heart of a child
you cannot escape the snares and quicksands
of this lying world.

# Dreams

Last night I had a wet dream.

My partner was a young woman lovely as pear-blossom, but she was not my wife, so it seemed like adultery. I felt very self-conscious on waking up.

One night recently I dreamed I had become the head of our Korean CIA. In daily life, if someone I meet says, 'You should try to get a good position in society,' I sometimes jokingly reply, 'Maybe I can become director of the CIA!' But this is too ridiculous!

Now I am getting on for 70, and I believe that after we part from our fishy-smelling bodies, like empty sea-shells along the shore, our life continues away from the waves; but although these are only dreams, is it all just some kind of child's foolishness? Or is it a sign of how deeply the Seven Sins are rooted within my subconscious?

I wonder if I shall ever get free of such fantasies, waking or dreaming?

# Shame Again

I wonder if you can even recall
what that thing called shame is like?

That something you first felt
when you began to be aware of things,
after you broke the vase
that mother had said 'Don't touch!'

like the day when Adam and Eve
covered their nakedness with fig-leaves
in the Garden of Eden
after they had picked and eaten the God-forbidden fruit.

Shame? What humans first felt
when they did any wrong,
a sign of human conscience,
an omen of human salvation.

But nowadays you grown-ups,
even when you do wrong, you feel no shame!

That's a sign your consciences are paralyzed,
an omen that you are heading towards destruction.

# Prayer

Those people know not
what they do.

These too know not
what they do.

Deliver us
from this blind strife.

Give us eyes to see
at least as much as two-week-old puppies can.

# Last Words

On the day the poet Gong-cho died
after completing his full life's span
in unhindered freedom without any concern
about each day's food or a place to rest,
as I was helping care for him

he left me these words:
'Freedom has shackled my whole existence!'

More significantly, Jesus of Nazareth,
who has shown me eternal life,
when he was dying nailed to the cross
truly fulfilling the will of Him,

cried out,
'My God, my God,
why have you forsaken me?'

Did those laments and cries of distress arise
from scepticism about their lives?
from uncertainty about their lives?
No! Certainly nothing like that at all!

But supposing there had been no such confessions,
they would merely have been people who lived
guided by their own fantasy,
sustained by their own persistence;
therefore those words are
a final affirming of their lives,
a final perfecting of their lives:

lives they lived as something offered up.

∗Note: Gong-cho was the pen-name of the poet O Sang-sun.

# Me

I am two of us inside.
Or maybe rather three.

The I that people see outside,
the I close hidden here inside,
and the unconscious I
that I myself cannot divine,
each I stands apart.

Today again: after a haircut and shave
in a local barber's shop
as the girl was giving me a massage
her hands touched my private parts
and for a moment there was a quarrel
between me wanting to warn her off with a 'Don't'
and me hoping her hands would slip that way again.

You can say that this kind of fight
between me and me inside is constant,
but recently one night in a dream
I was with a woman I'd never met
and it's ridiculous but I ejaculated;
who was the I acting there?

Which of these three, then,
is the real or false me,
the good or bad me,
which of them is really me?
The more I wonder the less I know.

And as I reflect this way and that,
I get more and more anxious
about which me will be involved
the day I die and go to be judged.

# Poetic Feeling

Each month for this series
I select bits of idle chatter such as this
and turn out things called poems,

so that one young poet, perhaps finding it rather odd,
observed, 'Then it seems there is absolutely nothing
in the whole world that is not a poem?'

Right! There is nothing
in the world, to be sure,
that is not a poem.

From humanity on down,
in every thing and every act,
all that is true and good and beautiful
is all poem.

More than that, in every person
and in every thing and in every act
the good, the beautiful, the true dwells.

And it is written that where sin increases
God's grace increases all the more.

Discovering that,
and then like a child
savoring and enjoying it,
is to be a poet.

*Note: 'Where sin increases... ': Romans 5:20.

# Eternity Today

# Myself

More than
the deep roots of every emotion,
big or small, of every kind,
that squirm and kick like little children
somewhere inside

and more than
the deep-sea fish
of six senses and seven sins,
that waves its tail
like a night-time shadow on a window pane

more, too, than
star-dust littering the yards
of Original Sin and Karma,
passing through the obscure darkness of the potter's kiln

and more than
the oasis spring gushing from the desert sand,
melting again into foam and flowing
after filtering through strata of origins and time
with their rustle of dry grass,
and the crack in the glacier, or even exploding particles

more, too, than
the world, itself smaller
than a millet seed
in the cosmic vastnesses

and more than

the ether — fullness of the boundless void
reaching beyond billions of light years
of starlight

more, too, than
the substantiality such fullness gives,
and more than its opposing nihility,
more, too, than unknown death

more, greater,
a soundless cosmic shout!
An immensity embracing Eternity!

Myself.

# Meditation

On the gleaming flank of an age-old rock,
lying like the eggs of some green insect,
fresh green moss is growing.

Is it just an effect of the springtime rain
that germinates the grain?
Or is it a return of infancy
in this centuries-old stone?

Here and now is an inevitable condition
where flowers, fruit,
and leaves too, are useless,
neither winds and rain,
nor thunder and lightning
are heard,
without distinction of day and night,
and knowing nothing of stench and perfume,
no separation of past, and real,
and dream.

Within the rock, no flow of filth, but
the brightness of a paper window in the morning sunlight!
In its communion with heaven's vastness,
accepting all the chaos of this world's variety-show,
by simply sitting there in silent meditation
it stills the ocean's tumult.

'But I am no Aladdin's lamp!'

Ah, moss so prudently clinging

to the indifferent rock!
True image of Meditation!

# In a Winter Orchard

In the orchard white with snow
like sprinkled salt,
a plum tree raises thick black branches
in a victory sign,
outlined with flowers in full bloom,
like an Easter garland.

'Behold, whoever puts his life in me,
even though he dies, will never die;
do not be doubtful
of invisible realities.'

Playfully, a single magpie
hops from branch to branch.

*

Beside a hole gaping
like a cavity in a lung,
stiff as a corpse
an apple tree lies, a full arm's girth.

A man comes by, dark as shade,
with a frame bound upon his back;
he lops the dead branches with an axe,
splits the trunk, and bears it all away.

'Behold, a figure of the dead
who will tomorrow be cast
into perdition's flames;

beware, then, lest the roots of your existence
become infected!'

A crow flies cawing
across the frozen sky.

# Midday Prayer

Take away this darkling veil that lies between myself and space.
Take away from off the earth all boundary lines, all fences and all walls.
Take away all human hatred, greed, and all discrimination.
Take away surrender and despair, both mine and theirs.

Restore again to me the gift of wonder, tears and prayer.
Restore again the dreams and loves of all the dead.
Restore again the hurts that human hands inflict on Nature.

And grant words to that rock, a face to this breeze,
and oh, to me grant to live eternally as a radiancy of purity.

# Within an Apple

Within a single apple's sphere
the clouds drift by.

Within a single apple's sphere
the good earth breathes.

Within a single apple's sphere
the river flows along.

Within a single apple's sphere
the sun blazes down.

Within a single apple's sphere
moon and stars whisper.

And within a single apple's sphere
our striving and our loving live eternal.

# In All Places

Are you within such stillness
as when, above a shimmering pond,
a dreamlike butterfly gently descends?

Are you obscurely there
in the desolate hills under rain,
their secluded places wrapped in darkness?

Are you like the compassion
appearing in hillside temple courts
where a flowering plantain's leaves
shelter a single rose-moss flower?

Are you found forlorn
beneath the bright hanging moon,
like shadows cast by a rooftop terrace?

Are you in some such height
as where chains of blue-tinged peaks
rise like screens around,
but above towers one snow-bright?

Are you in such perfect composure
as the long river timelessly flowing,
reflecting the sun and the moon?

Are you in the transparent frost
that unfolds on chill autumn mornings,
coating the naked branches?

Are you within that abundance
that undulates in the fields,
gold in the setting sun's slanting rays?

Are you too reduced to original silence,
like the soil ravaged by long winter's cold,
all fever spent?

Are you in such solemn power
as when the typhoon surges
and tidal waves race,
with clashes of lightning and thunder?

Are you as far removed
as the blending of vast blue immensity,
sea and sky made one
beyond all boundlessness?

Are you resplendent
as daybreak in the eastern sky,
high above the sevenfold rainbow's gleam,
like constellations' jewelled thrones?

Are you within the inborn joy
of swarms of fish flashing in jade-green streams
and the birds that chirp
while plum and peach delicately bloom?

Are you in the impassibility
of the mountain sheep
that nibbles grass then chews the cud,
looking up now at a cloud, now at a hill?

Are you in such spotless innocence

as shines in the eyes of a child
that gazes up at its mother and clasps
her breast through an open blouse?

Are you looking down on us
with the profound white-bearded smile
of drawings of Taoist Mountain Wizards?

You who fill all space and time,
whom I cannot serve under any such forms
but who resemble the white spaces in pictures
where the brush did not pass!

In no place confined,
by nothing defined,
everywhere present,
Lord God of all!

# Easter Hymn

On an old plum tree stump,
seemingly dead and rotten,
like a garland of victory
flowers gleam, dazzling.

Rooted in you, even in death
all things remain alive;
we see them reborn, transfigured.
How then could we doubt
our own Resurrection since
by your own you have given us proof?

Since there is your Resurrection and ours,
  Truth exists;
since there is your Resurrection and ours,
  Justice triumphs;
since there is your Resurrection and ours,
  suffering accepted has value;
since there is your Resurrection and ours,
  our faith, hope, love, are not in vain;
since there is your Resurrection and ours,
  our lives are not an empty abyss.

In this lost corner of the earth,
dappled by the spreading spring,
as I imagine that Day's world,
made perfect by our Resurrection,
I am overwhelmed in rapture.

# Mysterious Buds

The pitiless whirlwinds
have blown themselves out, and within me
mysterious buds have begun to grow.

What then is this freshness
touching my gaunt senses
that were dry as winter acacia trees?

All the things of creation,
once plunged in darkness,
turn into stars
and twinkling begin to shine;
until now locked in a tangled mesh,
my ideas flow free like thread from a skein.

Now there is nothing sad for me
about being born only to die;
all is just one aspect of eternity.

I still feel hungry if a meal is delayed,
my limbs still have rheumatic twinges,
nothing has changed, but within me
mysterious buds have begun to grow,
preparing to bloom with new flowers
once in Eternity's land.

# The True Appearance of the Word

As the cataract of ignorance falls
from off the eyesight of my soul,
I realize that all this huge Creation
round about me is the Word.

The hitherto quite unattended fact
that these familiar fingers number ten,
like the encounter with some miracle,
suddenly astonishes me

and the newly-opened forsythia flowers
in one corner of the hedge beyond my window
entrance me utterly,
like seeing a model of Resurrection.

Smaller than a grain of sand
in the oceanic vastness of the cosmos,
I realize that this my muttering,
by a mysterious grace of the Word,

is no imagined thing, no mere sign,
but Reality itself.

# Jesus of Nazareth

Jesus of Nazareth!
Who are you really?

Born in a stable's manger,
dying nailed to a cross with thieves,
the unlucky possessor of an absurd destiny.

Wandering around, without house or home,
you kept company with low class people,
with prostitutes and rebels,
with louts from other regions
normally considered enemies;
you enjoyed eating and drinking with them.

To the poor,
to the hungry,
to those in tears,
to those despised for their just deeds,
insulted, driven out, and dishonored
for having practiced what is right,
you dared to proclaim:
'You, you are the blessed!
Yours, yours is the Kingdom of God!'

You gave sight to the blind,
you opened the deaf man's ears,
you made the cripple walk,
you completely healed the leper's sores,
you brought the dead back to life,

as you yourself said,
heaped with the whole world's hatred,
insulted and driven out,
finally labelled a traitor
and dying without any show,
you are the ultimate failure

and to me, united with you from my mother's womb,
you are the very ground of my being, the way
from which, at times, I incline to stray,
finding it a nuisance,
at times a cause of discouragement, despair;
at times, although extremely familiar,
you look like an absolute stranger.

*

So what on earth are you really like?

You were not a thinker,
you were not a moralist,
you were not one of this world's statesmen,
and you were not the founder of a religion.

Therefore, you did not teach any kind of learning,
you did not teach any kind of rules,
you did not launch any kind of social reform movement,
neither did you teach some kind of detachment from this world.
You did not compute
anyone's past merit, or lack of it,
you did not compute
anyone's past sins, whether many or few.
Really, you overturned the thoughts and words

of everyone in the world:
'Come to me, all you
who are toiling and struggling along
under heavy burdens,
I will give you rest!'
To suffering humanity
you proclaimed liberation,

and you taught that God is our Father,
that he is Love itself, infinite,
that when, nestling like children in his breast,
we forgive as our Father forgives,
and love as our father loves,
then eternal bliss dwells in our lives,
and that, you taught, is called 'the Kingdom of God'
and having practiced at the cost of your life
the sincerity of such loving,
you bore witness by your Resurrection
to that Love's imperishability.

# Knots 28.

From Daejeon we skirted Geumsan,
and then, as we left the Yeongdong highway
we came under attack from a Communist guerilla unit.

Hastily abandoning the jeep I was in,
I crouched behind the bank of a field beside the road
and pointed the M1 rifle I had never once fired
in the direction of the enemy.

Just then I noticed the seeds from a dried dandelion
right before my eyes being carried away in a gust of wind.

The question:
'Now once my flesh is scattered like that,
where will the seeds of my life go
to give birth to new flowers?'

and the realization that
'I am eternally wrapped in a profound mystery.'

came to my mind in a flash,
making all fear and apprehension vanish
and drawing me into a rapture I cannot name.

# Knots 70.

In a pause between the chanting of Buddhist monks,
a group of Catholic sisters, looking like wild chrysanthemums
blooming in a mountainside radish field,
kneeling before the departed soul of the Venerable Hyobong
are reciting together the prayers for the dead.

— Lord, grant this departed soul repose.
— And may light eternal shine upon him.

What blessed spectacle is this?
What dazzling marvel?

Two faiths that reject each other as wrong teaching, false way,
stand in opposition, calling each other superstition, evil,
each seeing the other as a brood of snakes or scorpions

and here the gates of mutual succor stand open!

Humans, do not divide
the truth that is only one.

Humans, do not divide God,
who is only one.

Hearing this report on the radio
I was overjoyed, so overjoyed I sobbed.

∗Note: The Venerable Hyobong was one of the most famed monks of his generation. He died in 1965. This poem reflects my joy at the openness toward other religions contained in the documents that emerged from the Second Vatican Council (1962-5).

# Knots 76.

A torso like a ripe peach.

A butterfly
fallen in ecstasy on a flowery tomb.

A tongue with the perfume of melons.

A seagull plunging
into blue waves that flash white teeth.

In a gaze fixed on the distant horizon.

A roe deer
drinking at a secret spring in a virgin forest.

Abyss of Eros,
beauty of original sin

*

The purring cat's deceitful, mysterious
face.

Venus' neck
spun about with hempen locks.

On velvet breasts the imprint of a hawk's claws.

An hour-glass navel.

Buttocks smooth wooden bowls,
secret flesh of tree-trunk thighs.

The narrowing rapids of a rendezvous,
a grassy bank aflame on a spring day.

In primitive darkness,

beneath an azalea-cliff blanket
a naked woman
on a foaming, lapping wave-white sheet
joins her arms
like the cords
that criminals are bound with

........

The cooing of doves.

Breath-taking moment, oh, mystery!

*

I draw in empty space.

That face,
that voice,
that smile,
those thighs,

but that love
cannot be drawn.

Things drawn in the heart

may not be given form.

*

With that hand
that caressed her naked body
I stroke my gray beard.

Passion faded into pale silver...

That loving, riding the bucket,
has been drawn up to the heavens.

Henceforth, all those times and places
are one with Eternity.

# Knots 81.

Like a two-week-old puppy
my eyes are open to God's spirit.

All things in the universe, hitherto so faded,
now emit beams of grace
while their transience, as they pass from birth to death,
that before was a source of regret and sorrow
proves now to be simply one image of eternity.

Now Heaven is not something feeding and clothing
only birds and flowers
and I give thanks with tears
that it sustains and quickens me with its efforts.

The way the sun rises in the east when morning comes
and sets in the west when evening comes,
and when the proper time is past I feel hungry
may always be the same,

within my consciousness, previously devoid of any entrance,
limitless time and space have opened
and everything is new
everything is precious
everything is beautiful.

# Knots 86.

Lying under a white sheet,
I am carried off in an ambulance.

The evening sky hangs upside-down beneath my feet,
forming a terrible quagmire of death.

I picture my corpse like this, rigid, stretched out,
a skeleton, decomposed, reduced to dust.

Behind me, a lifetime lies smothered in error,
I have not even managed to bear buds of sweat and tears,
let alone the love that can blossom in Eternity.

No point in getting flustered now...

'Father, into your hands
I commend my spirit.'

Instinctively repeating the last words of Him
whom I have only aped, not truly served,
I sever the link with all concepts.

And my breath becomes rasping.

* Note: In early 1979, an attack of asthma nearly killed me.

# Fields 58.

I have never so far heard
any voice whatever,
from heaven, from earth,
or from men.

Neither have I seen any vision.

Within my breast have blossomed and vanished
billions
upon billions of tales of things endured
but I could not express a single word.

# Fields 59.

Was my soul born, from the very start,
with unseeing eyes?

Day after day, every day
I open wide the eyes of my being
and look up to heaven
but encounter only obscurity, only vast emptiness...

# Fields 60.

Just one footstep ahead of us,
no, from the very beginning,
with the solar system turning and turning,
you, field,
have been swimming on through space.

# River 14.

The river flows on,
without a filthy heart,
all pure of body,
it flows like time in Eternity.

The river flows on,
without a paltry body,
all pure of heart,
it flows like Eternity in time.

The river flows on,
neither heart nor body,
it flows, an essence of nothingness.

# River 41.

I now have become one drop of water
and flow into the stream.

I now have awoken from the dream
that served as the very thread of life,
I now have emerged from all the real
that served by yearning to attach me to life

now I am released from time
now I am released from me.

I now have lost the form of me
there is no I to call me me
this river that shows no beginning no end
is simply I.

Now as I freely flow along
within an immutable order,
I experience the origin and end
of all created beings.

# Wings

When I first began to toddle
the very first thing I felt
was the fact that my legs and arms
would not move just as I wanted them to.

And now I am close on seventy
what once again I feel
is the fact that my legs and arms
will not move just as I want them to.

Once I would totter towards
my mother's outstretched hands
and now as I live gasp by gasp
clinging to unseen outstretched hands

what I am hoping and longing for is
not a jet plane
or a spaceship

but an experience of the ecstasy of donning wings,
like a caterpillar as it becomes a butterfly,
and, joining with the angels, to fly and fly
with the whole cosmos as my flowery field:
that ecstasy.

# Lord! Once Again

1.

Lord!
Once again this midday my soul
wandering in search of your kingdom
like a kite soaring through the air
when the cord is snapped by a twirling blast
has vanished into the blue.

2.

Lord!
Once again this evening my soul
like a puppy that gazes up at the moon
and barks
is barking and whimpering towards you
and gets no reply.

# The Baby Now

The baby now
is seeing something.
Is hearing something.
Is thinking something.

It's seeing forms like those when
Mohammed in the cave on Mount Hira
received revelation from God.

It's hearing voices like that which
rang out over the head of Jesus of Nazareth
when he was baptized on the banks of the Jordan.

It's lost in thoughts like those when
Shakyamuni attained enlightenment sitting
beneath the Bo tree in the forests of Mount Gaya.

No, the baby is seeing, hearing, thinking
something that is none of those.

It's seeing, hearing, thinking something
that no one else can see or hear or think:

something that as a quite unique human being
it alone will have to bring to bud and blossom.

And all on its own it's smiling sweetly.

# Hole in the Heart

Somewhere deep inside my heart
a hole has opened

so that as I touch
that emptiness or rather
that boundlessness
that eternity

out of that place
that can only be called
the Void

a miraculous breeze comes blowing.
A mysterious sound comes chiming.
A divine word comes ringing.

And as I, becoming a baby again,
respond
with pre-verbal language,

as everything in the whole world,
each in its own place and with its own form,
becomes a bright star and shines,

as I experience my immortality,
the transience of life grows more precious still
and I am most utterly happy!

# With Wild Flowers

In a flower-pot out on my veranda
where orchids had died off
a wild plant came up of its own accord
and produced flowers like white dust.

This single tiny plant,
occupying this moment in eternity
occupying this place in infinity:
the fact that it has born flowers,
the more I think about it,
the more it seems mysterious beyond measure.

Indeed, this being called I too,
occupying this moment in eternity
occupying this place in infinity:
the fact that I am face to face with this wild flower,
the more I think about it,
the more it too seems mysterious beyond measure.

And finally as I muse over these things I,
escaping from the being called I
and united with the wild flower

as one expression of eternity and infinity,
as one part of eternity and infinity,
as one love of eternity and infinity,

now exist here.

# Eternity Within

1.

Day and night, inside the confines
within me, snarling,

I wonder what that ferocious beast
is really like?

Has it glimpsed some prey?
Today it is bounding high.

2.

Aimlessly drifting
over the sea within me,

I wonder where is the port of call
of that anchorless skiff?

The waves seem rough.
Today it is rocking wildly.

3.

Endlessly stretching its pinions
in the vastnesses within me,

I wonder when and where

that bluebird dream will be fulfilled?

It longs for the Gardens of Immortality.
Today Eternity lies within me.

# Today

Today again I confront a day that is source of mystery.

In this day the past, present and future are one,
just as each drop of water in that river
is linked to a tiny spring in some mountain valley
and linked to the distant, azure sea.

In that way, in this today of mine, being linked to eternity,
at this very moment I am living that eternity.

That means that it is not after I have died
but from today on that I must live eternity,
must live a life worthy of eternity.

I must live in poverty of heart.
I must live with an empty heart.

Ku Sang as a university student in Tokyo (early 1940s)

Ku Sang as a journalist in Daegu right after the Korean War (early and mid 1950s)

At an international event for writers in Tokyo, Japan (late 1950s)

At a ceremony awarding prizes for poets (mid 1960s)

At his house in Waegwan, Ku Sang poses with a pumpkin that he has gathered in his own garden in his hands. (late 1960s)

In Vietnam with writers following the Army (late 1960s)

At a ceremony with Cardinal Kim Su-hwan, the poet Kim Nam-jo and sisters (late 1960s)

Ku Sang as exchange professor at Hawaii University lecturing on "comparative culture between the East and the West" (early 1970s)

At the house of the painter Kim Gi-chang (penname Unbo) (early 1980s)

At the unveiling ceremony of a monument inscribed with a poem beside the Han River (early 1990s)

In his study (early 1990s)

In his living room (early 1990s)

In his study (mid 1990s)

In his study (mid 1990s)